A Child's First Library of Learning

Weather

TIME-LIFE BOOKS • AMSTERDAM

Contents

Why Do Clouds Form?

ANSWER The sun warms the water in the ocean, in rivers and in the ground. As the water gets warmer it turns into a gas called water vapour. We cannot see it, but water vapour is rising into the sky all around us. After it rises, the water vapour cools. Then it turns into droplets of water and tiny bits of ice. When enough droplets and bits of ice come together, clouds are formed.

A Storm Cloud Forms

Water droplets

Water vapour

▲ A fleecy white cloud appears.

▲ More and more water vapour rises into the air, and the cloud grows larger and larger.

▲ The water droplets and ice in the cloud are forced upwards. This produces a storm, or cumulo-nimbus cloud.

5

❓ Why Do Clouds Have Different Shapes?

ANSWER Clouds form different shapes depending upon how high up they are. High in the sky they look like feathery white threads. Lower down they form into fleecy clouds, like fluffy cotton wool. But height isn't the only thing that matters. The wind forms clouds into many different shapes, too.

Cirro-cumulus clouds look like the scales of a fish.

Cirrus clouds are feathery, as if they'd been swept.

Cloud caps often form around the tops of mountains.

Why Are Some Clouds Darker Than Others?

ANSWER Some clouds are thin and others are thick. Because sunlight easily passes through thin clouds, they appear bright or white. Light can't pass through thick clouds so easily. The parts where light passes through will appear white, but the thick parts where the light doesn't pass through will look grey or black.

The tops of the clouds are white!

Above the clouds

△ Below the clouds

Then Why Are Clouds Red in the Evening?

Sometimes at sunset dust in the air makes the sun look red. So clouds look red too.

▲ Clouds turn red in the light of the sunset.

Clouds can turn other colours too

▲ These clouds shine like gold.

▲ These clouds look purple.

❓ Why Does it Rain?

ANSWER Clouds are filled with water. Rain clouds have more water than they can hold. When a cloud has too much water, it rains.

I wish it would rain.

Look! It's getting cloudy.

▲ These are rain clouds. It's going to rain soon.

▲ Plants and frogs love the rain.

Tell Me, What's It Like Inside a Rain Cloud?

Rain clouds are made up of many water droplets and small bits or particles of ice. When the particles get heavy enough they start to fall towards the earth. They gather water around them as they fall. The ice particles grow larger, and then they melt and fall to earth as rain.

• To the Parent

In misty rain the drops are about 0.1 to 0.2 mm in diameter, while ordinary raindrops are about 1.0 mm. In a heavy rain, drops may measure 5 to 6 mm. An estimated one million water droplets in a cloud form just one raindrop. In light clouds the drops seldom become heavy enough to fall to the ground.

❓ Where Does the Rain Go?

ANSWER Rainwater flows to lower ground, running along ditches and into sewers. Some of it sinks into the earth, where trees and plants will take it in. Some of it stays on the ground in puddles. But puddles disappear as the water sinks into the ground or rises into the air as water vapour.

A sewer pipe

● **To the Parent**

Some rainwater collects in puddles, some sinks into the earth, and some flows into streams and rivers, eventually reaching the sea. Water that goes underground may emerge later and flow into streams. Much of the rainwater left on the surface of the ground evaporates into the atmosphere.

After the rain stops, make paths for the rainwater to flow in. The water will flow to lower ground.

Dig a hole in the wet ground and see how far you have to dig before a pool forms.

Water that sinks into the earth flows downwards along cracks in the ground.

Sept. 2016 age 9.

❓ What is a Monsoon?

ANSWER A monsoon is a strong wind that brings heavy rain. In many Asian countries during the monsoon season this wind carries warm air currents from the tropics. The warm air tries to push out the cool air. It pushes so hard that it rises high into the sky. There's a lot of water vapour in the warm air, so it forms more and more rain clouds. Finally the rain pours down from those clouds.

Cold winds

Ooh, it's so cold!

I'm Freezing. Shiver!

What takes place during the monsoon?

▲ Rice is planted. Because there's so much rain, the young rice plants grow very fast.

▲ When there's a lot of rain, rivers overflow their banks, and cliffs and hillsides come sliding down.

14

Above the clouds it's clear.

Warm winds

Ooh, it's so hot!

The warm winds bring the summer

When the warm air finally drives out the cool air, the rain stops. Then there are lots of fine, sunshiny days.

◀ When a lot of rain falls, the air is very humid. Mould forms easily and food spoils quickly.

▲ Snails and frogs love the rain. Many animals are very active during the monsoon season.

Sudden Showers

? Why do Squalls Hit So Suddenly?

ANSWER Sudden showers or squalls come from cumulo-nimbus clouds. That kind of cloud moves across the sky very quickly. One minute it may look clear, and the next moment the clouds have moved in. That's why summer showers often come down unexpectedly.

Hey!
It's raining!

Hey!

Clouds That Bring Rain

Cumulo-nimbus clouds
Cumulo-nimbus clouds often move as fast as a car. They bring sudden showers.

Nimbo-stratus clouds
As nimbo-stratus clouds move in, the sky gets darker gradually, not all of a sudden.

◀ Clouds that bring drizzle

What Is Lightning?

As thunderclouds swell, electricity builds up. Sometimes you can see a spark of electricity jumping from one cloud to another. And when it jumps to earth there's a flash of lightning.

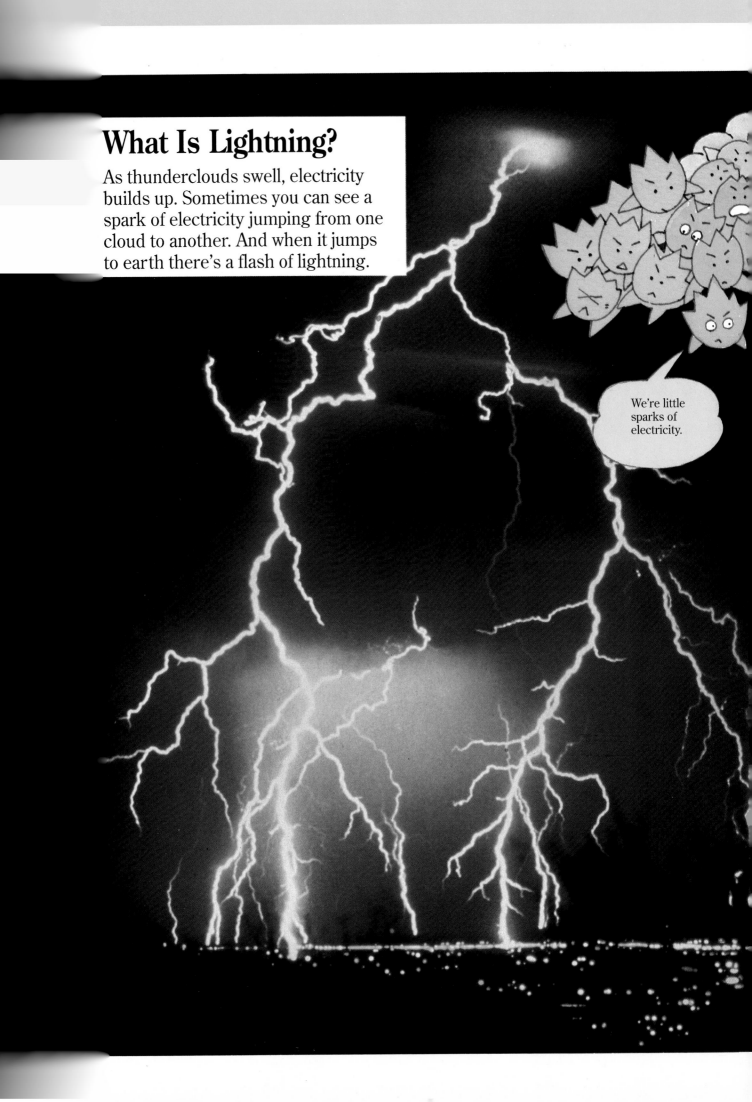

We're little sparks of electricity.

■ Electric train sparks

When an electric train runs on overhead wires at night you can see sparks jumping between the train and the power lines. Those sparks are electricity. Lightning is caused by the same kind of spark.

▲ Cumulo-nimbus clouds, which cause lightning.

● **To the Parent**

Thunderclouds develop from cumulo-nimbus clouds. Electricity is built up inside the clouds and then is suddenly discharged into the air. Known as lightning, the discharged electricity has an enormous force: as much as several million volts.

❓ Why Does Thunder Rumble?

ANSWER As you know, the movement of electricity inside clouds causes lightning. That movement presses and bumps against the air around it, and that produces sound. The air that was disturbed first then bumps against the air next to it, and so on. That produces the rolling rumble of thunder.

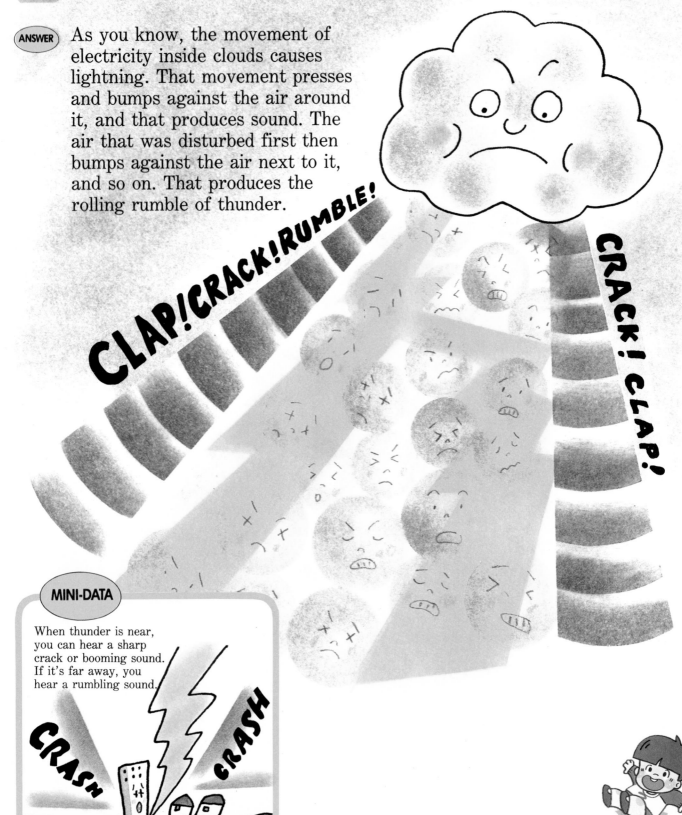

CLAP!CRACK!RUMBLE!

CRACK! CLAP!

MINI-DATA

When thunder is near, you can hear a sharp crack or booming sound. If it's far away, you hear a rumbling sound.

CRASH

CRASH

20

Why Don't the Thunder and Lightning Come Together?

If lightning is very close you hear the thunder at almost the same time. But if it's far away the sound of the thunder comes a few seconds later. That's because light travels much, much faster than sound.

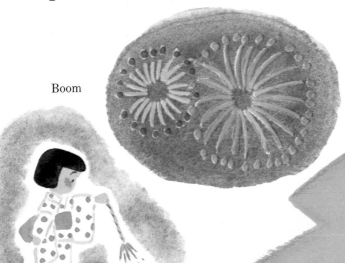

Boom

When a sparkler is lit you see the sparks and hear the sound at the same time. But when you watch a fireworks display you see the light before you hear the sound.

Wow!

Rumble, rumble

MINI-DATA

In Japan, long ago, people used to believe that there was a Thunder God who lived in the clouds and made thunder. They believed that he was always looking for children's navels. If he saw one, he would fly down to earth and steal it! So children were told to cover their navels if they were out of doors during a thunderstorm.

21

❓ Where Does Lightning Strike?

ANSWER Lightning usually strikes tall objects like buildings and trees. Lightning will also strike metal objects, even, occasionally, the metal tip of an umbrella. If you're playing in an open field or park where there are no tall objects, you should go inside if thunderclouds appear. If you're swimming, get out right away.

Lightning will strike power lines and towers.

Places where lightning is a danger

In an open field where you may be the tallest thing around.

Near tall trees.

High on a hill or mountain.

Lightning rods. The rod on top of this country church passes the electricity in lightning into the ground without hurting anyone.

A tree struck by lightning may be snapped off like this or burnt.

Places that are safe

Most large buildings are protected by lightning rods, so you're safe inside.

Lightning doesn't usually strike vehicles, like cars and buses, if the doors and windows are closed.

❓ **Why Does It Snow?**

ANSWER Clouds contain water vapour and tiny ice particles. When it's very cold the water vapour near the ice particles freezes. The particles get heavier and start falling. If the air on the way down is warm, the ice particles melt and turn into rain. If the air is cold, they stay frozen and fall to the ground as snow.

Ice Particles

Snowflakes

If it's cold, the snow doesn't melt as it falls.

If it's warm, the snow melts and falls as rain.

24

Why Does Snow Look White?

Light is reflected in all directions when it hits snow. That's why the snow looks white. Light bounces off white paper in the same way.

TRY THIS

Put some white paper and some black paper out in the sunlight. The white paper reflects the sunlight in all directions. It's really bright and dazzling. But the black paper doesn't reflect light. It's not at all dazzling.

Sept. 2016   age 9.

Did You Know What Pretty Shapes the Snowflake Have?

ANSWER Snowflakes, or particles of snow, have beautiful shapes and forms. The particles are called crystals. Snow crystals come in many shapes. When they form, the shape depends on how much moisture is in the air and on how cold the air is.

The photographs in the circles show crystals of snow. As you can see, their shapes are very different.

Large snowflakes and small snowflakes

Sometimes snowflakes are large and sometimes they're small. When it's cold, snowflakes are usually small. But when it's warmer, snowflakes start to melt. They join other snowflakes and lose their fine shape. Many small ones stick together to form larger flakes.

That's why sleet has such large snowflakes in it.

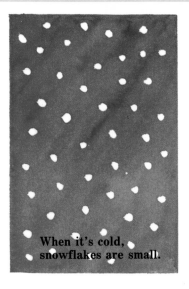

When it's cold, snowflakes are small.

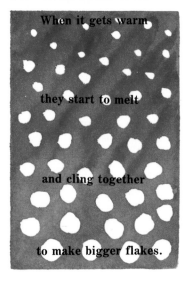

When it gets warm

they start to melt

and cling together

to make bigger flakes.

26

Snow crystals

Let's look at crystals of snow

■ What you need

Put them outside
so they'll
be cold.

Magnifying glass

Black paper
or cloth

Snowflakes will melt
if you breathe on
them, so cover your
mouth and nose with
a mask like this.

If snowflakes get
warm, they'll melt.
Wear gloves so
that won't happen.

Catch the snow as it
falls onto the black
paper or cloth. Then
you can look at it with
the magnifying glass.

• To the Parent

The existence of snow crystals has been known for more than
400 years. There is a great variety in the structure of snow
crystals, depending upon the temperature and pressure of the
upper air where they form. Now that it is possible to create
snow crystals in the laboratory, the temperature and humidity
conditions in the upper atmosphere can be determined from the
study and analysis of the crystal structure of the falling snow.

Why Does It Snow More on One Side of Mountains?

ANSWER In winter, cold winds blow from the sea to the land. They bring clouds that rise up the mountainside. The tops of the mountains are cold and cool the clouds. When that happens, snow falls on the side of the mountains facing the sea. On the other side, the weather is dry.

In places that have a lot of snow, you sometimes see snow piled all the way to the roof.

The clouds that brought snow to one side of the mountain disappear as they come down the other side.

● To the Parent

Cold winter winds blow across the northern oceans and pick up large amounts of water vapour. When they reach land, the clouds come into contact with mountains, rise and become even colder. Most of the water vapour picked up over the ocean falls at this time as snow. When the winds come down on the opposite side of the mountain the moisture is depleted, so the snow stops, the clouds vanish and the weather is fine.

? Why Do Icicles Form?

ANSWER When snow piles up on the roof of a house, the snow at the bottom gradually melts and runs down the roof. As the water drips over the side, it comes into the cold air and freezes again. This makes small icicles. As more water runs down the icicles it freezes on top of the old ice, and the icicles get longer and longer.

▲ Icicles formed on the edge of a roof

Can't I play too?

On guard!

■ How icicles form

The heat inside the house passes through the roof and melts the piled-up snow.

As the snow melts, the water gets cold and freezes again.

Icicles grow longer as the water melts and freezes again and again.

▲ When a waterfall freezes, lots of icicles are formed.

▲ Water has dripped inside a tunnel and formed these icicles. They hang from the tunnel's ceiling.

● **To the Parent**

Because icicles are frozen run-off water, they form not only on the eaves of houses but also on stones near the outlets of springs, on the roofs of tunnels and around waterfalls. When snow is melted by the heat in a house or the warmth of the sun and the run-off water then refreezes, icicles form.

What Are Frost Pillars?

ANSWER When it gets very cold, the surface of the ground may freeze. The water under the surface is drawn up towards the ice. That pushes the ice upwards. The water that was moving up then freezes. As this happens again and again, columns, or frost pillars, form.

▲ **Towers of strength.** Frost pillars have unbelievable power as they push upwards.

■ How frost pillars form

The water on the surface freezes, and the water underneath is pulled up.

The water on the surface freezes, and the water underneath is pulled up.

The water that has moved up freezes, and more water is drawn upwards.

Well, Then, Why Does Frost Form?

There's a lot of water vapour in the air. On cold winter mornings, rocks and leaves are chilled. The water vapour freezes when it gets near those cold rocks and leaves. When it freezes, it turns into ice forms called frost.

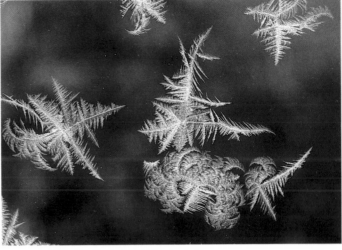

▲ You can see beautiful patterns of ice in the frost that forms on window glass.

Water vapour

Frost

▲ Frost on leaves

The pointed ends of the frost can be seen with a magnifying glass.

TRY THIS

Open the door of the refrigerator and look in the freezer. Part of it is white inside. In the air in the room there's water vapour. Whenever you open the refrigerator, some air gets in, and the water vapour in the air turns to ice.

● **To the Parent**

Pillars of ground frost form as water in the ground freezes. If the particles of soil are too small or large, as in clay or sand, the capillary action that brings water to the surface can not take place and frost pillars do not form. Automatic defrosters prevent water vapour in air from forming frost in refrigerators.

33

Why Does Ice Form?

ANSWER On cold mornings, ponds and puddles may freeze. Water turns to ice when the temperature drops to zero degrees Celsius. When the sun comes up and it gets warmer the ice will gradually melt.

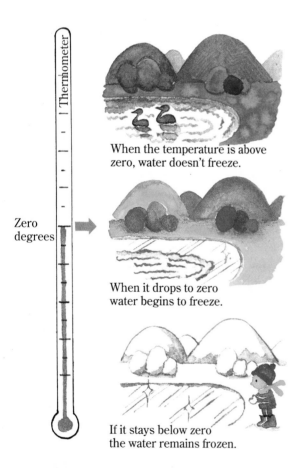

Thermometer

Zero degrees

When the temperature is above zero, water doesn't freeze.

When it drops to zero water begins to freeze.

If it stays below zero the water remains frozen.

▲ This is from water that froze in a bucket.

▲ **A frozen lake.** In countries that have cold winters people can go ice skating on the thick layer of ice that forms on lakes.

▲ **A frozen sea.** If it gets cold enough even seawater will freeze. The wind blows the ice south, and it covers the sea's surface.

?What Makes Ice Melt?

ANSWER When ice is warmed, it
melts and turns into water
again. Let's see some of
the ways we can melt it.

Having some fun with ice

Breathe through a straw
onto a piece of ice.
Because your breath is
warm, it will gradually
make a hole in the ice.

Ice cubes will stick
together if you put
salt on them.

If ice is in direct sunlight it melts more quickly.

If a warm breeze blows on ice the ice will start to melt.

I see! If ice is in the shade it won't melt so quickly.

Put several different kinds of things on top of a block of ice. The heavier a thing is the more it pushes down on the ice and melts it. Gradually the object will sink into the ice as it melts.

Why Can We Slide on the Ice?

ANSWER When we walk on the ice it melts a little under our feet. The water from the melted ice is what lets us slide. It's almost the same as when you put wax or oil on a floor. You can slide more easily. Snow is also slippery because its surface melts and forms water. People in cold countries can have fun sliding on ice and snow.

MINI-DATA

Ice skates are made in a special way so they'll slide better. You can slide in leather shoes too, or in any shoes that have a flat bottom. But the soles of boots are rough, so they won't slide very well.

Ice skates

Straw boots

Leather shoes

Rubber-soled boots

With straw on my shoes I won't slip.

• To the Parent

If you hold a piece of ice in your hand long enough, it will gradually slip away. The surface of the ice will melt from just the heat of your hand, and the film of water acts as a lubricant. Friction and pressure also melt ice when we walk on it, and that is why we slide even when it is below zero.

❓ Why Does Fog Form?

ANSWER Fog is like a cloud that forms near the ground. It forms when warmer moist air passes over cool ground. When that happens, the air cools and water vapour turns to droplets. That's what makes fog. We often see fog in the morning because the ground has become cold during the night.

The air contains water vapour, a gas made up of tiny, tiny droplets of water, so small that you cannot see them. They are called molecules. When water vapour cools it forms droplets of water, still tiny, but you can see them. These droplets are called mist.

Warm air

Water droplets

Water vapour

Cold ground

• To the Parent

Clouds and fog are formed when the water vapour in the air condenses into water droplets. When this happens high up in the sky, clouds are formed. When the condensation occurs at ground level, fog is created. Another difference is that the water droplets in clouds are much larger than those in fog. Fogs vary in density; a thin fog is called a mist.

40

Fog forms in places like these and in many others

▲ Over cold ocean water it can even hide big steamships.

▲ It makes driving dangerous on highways in low places.

What Is Wind?

ANSWER Wind is air that is moving. If you wave a fan it makes a breeze. And if you pedal a tricycle as fast as you can you'll feel wind in your face. With the fan you move the air, but on a tricycle you move yourself through the air. The air seems to be moving, just like wind blowing when the weather changes.

Why Does the Wind Blow?

When air is heated by the sun, it rises. Then cold air flows in to take the place of the air that rose. The sun heats the cold air and it rises too, and more cold air flows in behind it. This flow of air is what creates wind.

Cool air

Warm air

• To the Parent

Air expands when it is heated. The air that has expanded is lighter, and it rises. When this happens, the air pressure drops because there is less air. The cooler surrounding air rushes into the low pressure area. The rush of air is what wind is. Air contracts when it is cooled. Air that has risen is cooled. It contracts, becomes heavier, and descends to the earth, where it is heated to rise again. This flow of warm air upwards and cool air downwards is called convection.

Why Are Some Winds So Cold?

ANSWER In the winter, countries in the far north become very, very cold. Cold winds come from those northern lands and bring freezing temperatures with them. When these winds reach you, it is a sure sign that winter has arrived.

Cold north wind

Gosh, it's cold!

And How Long Does the Cold Last?

In the early spring, warm winds from the south grow stronger. They drive away the cold, wintry winds. When they do that the coldest days of winter are over.

Cold north wind

It's warm!

Warm south winds

● **To the Parent**

In some countries, winds change from season to season and are called seasonal winds. In Japan, for instance, northwesterly winds from the Asian mainland arrive in winter; in summer there is a southwesterly wind off the Pacific. In Europe, winds change all year round, but westerly winds tend to predominate.

❓ What Makes Hurricanes Form?

ANSWER Hurricanes form in warm ocean waters. As you know, warm water turns into water vapour quickly. Lots of water vapour rises from the warm seas. It enters the air, rises and forms cumulo-nimbus clouds. Strong winds blow the clouds into swirls. As the clouds get more and more water vapour from the sea, they become larger. That's how a hurricane forms.

When more and more water vapour comes together, cumulo-nimbus clouds are created.

When water vapour cools, clouds form.

The water in the sea gets warm.

There is a strong swirl of wind in the cumulo-nimbus cloud.

The swirl of wind grows as it takes on lots of water vapour from the sea.

MINI-DATA

Did you know that hurricanes and typhoons are the same kind of storm?

Hurricanes form in the Atlantic, typhoons in the Pacific and Indian Oceans. Some parts of China and South East Asia have typhoons in summer. Japan has more in autumn.

Summer path

Autumn path

Spring path

● **To the Parent**

A hurricane or typhoon is a tropical cyclone in which winds attain speeds greater than 120 kilometres per hour. Sometimes, they cause extensive damage. The hurricane season in the northern hemisphere runs from late June to October. During that time, three to four hurricanes will strike the eastern coast of the United States. As many as 30 typhoons form in the Pacific and Indian Oceans.

What Is a Typhoon's Eye?

ANSWER

A typhoon, like a hurricane, is a lot of clouds swirling around in a circle. In the centre are very few clouds. If you looked down from above, you'd see a hole, like an eye, in the middle of the clouds. That's why a typhoon's centre is called the eye.

There are clouds all around the eye of the typhoon. The small dark place is the eye.

In a hurricane or typhoon's eye there are no clouds and very little wind. No rain falls in the part called the eye.

TRY THIS

Stir the water in a basin round and round with your hand. See how a whirlpool forms in the water? In the centre is an eye that's lower than the rest of the water.

Oh! There's an eye!

Look down on the water in the basin and you'll see an eye in the centre. It will be the low part of the water.

This photograph was taken by a weather satellite.

●To the Parent

In the northern hemisphere, hurricanes and typhoons turn in an anticlockwise direction. The centre has no clouds. This centre, which is produced by a strong downdraught, is called the eye, and it may be as much as 30 to 50 kilometres in diameter in a fully developed hurricane or typhoon.

Why Do Hurricanes Bring Heavy Rains?

ANSWER Inside a hurricane are a lot of rain clouds, and they bring the heavy rain.

▲ Sometimes sudden hard rains cause severe flooding. These boys in a German town brave floodwaters on their bikes.

When a storm is near, the sky is covered with rain clouds.

Why Does the Wind Blow So Hard During a Hurricane?

Near the centre of a hurricane the air is pushed up with great force. When that happens other air rushes in to take its place. That's why the wind is strong.

▲ Strong winds make high ocean waves crash against the shore.

● **To the Parent**

The heavy rains of a hurricane come from cumulo-nimbus clouds near the storm's centre. The total rainfall from one hurricane can be as much as 500 million to 4,000 million tonnes of water. To understand what an immense volume that is, consider that a reservoir for a metropolis of 15 million people may hold less than 200 million tonnes. Hurricanes are accompanied by strong winds that can knock down trees and demolish houses.

Why Do Kites Fly?

ANSWER A kite rises into the air when the wind blows against it. But the wind has to keep blowing with the same strength. If it doesn't, the kite will come circling back down to the ground.

Then What's the Best Way to Fly a Kite?

Adjust the length of your string according to how hard the wind is blowing. And make the upper string a little shorter than the lower one.

Run against the wind with the kite.

If the kite spins, put a tail on it.

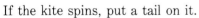

Why Does the Weather Change?

ANSWER High up in the sky, the wind is always blowing and clouds are always moving with that wind. As the clouds move across the sky, the weather changes. So it's really the wind that brings rainy or cloudy weather.

Let me help too.

Oh, it's getting cloudy.

● **To the Parent**

There are air currents in the sky that flow from west to east. The most powerful of these are the jet streams, which reach speeds as high as 130 metres per second, or 470 kph. These air currents carry low and high pressure areas along with them, so that changes in the weather move from west to east.

Did You Know That a Red Sunset Is a Sign of Fine Weather?

ANSWER The clouds that bring rain or hide the sun come from the direction where the sun sets. If there are no clouds in that direction the sunset will be bright red. So if you see a brilliant red sunset you know there will probably be fine weather the next day.

Here there are rain clouds in the direction where the sun sets, and the sun's rays are hidden.

Here there are no rain clouds in the direction where the sun sets, and the light is bright red and clear.

Why Do We Have Rain Even Though the Sun Is Shining?

ANSWER Sometimes it rains even when it's sunny and there aren't any clouds around. We call this a sun-shower. Strong winds bring the rain from clouds that are far away. Sometimes a sun-shower is rain that falls from very high clouds. The clouds disappear before the rain can reach the ground.

But Why Do Clouds Disappear?

Clouds don't often disappear just because they have turned into rain. When they disappear it's usually because the wind has carried them downwards and they have turned into water vapour.

Look! The clouds have gone.

MINI-DATA

Clouds can float upwards on winds that blow from low to high. When the wind stops, the clouds gradually come down again.

● **To the Parent**

Rain that falls when it is sunny and there are no clouds in sight is called a sun-shower. It may come from distant clouds and be carried on strong winds, or after the raindrops have formed the weather may change suddenly, causing the clouds to disappear. Clouds form where there is an updraught of air. When this updraught ceases, the cloud particles fall gradually. If a downdraught carries the particles to a lower level where it is warmer, the particles will change back into their invisible form of water vapour.

Why Do Rainbows Form?

ANSWER You've noticed, of course, that you don't see rainbows at night. And you don't see them on cloudy days or when it's raining. Rainbows appear when it clears up after the rain or during a sun-shower. We see a rainbow when the sun's light is reflected from water droplets in the air.

TRY THIS

On a fine day you can make your own rainbow.

▲ With the sun behind you, spray some water out of a spray bottle. You'll make a rainbow.

▲ When you make a soap bubble, you can see the colours of the rainbow in it.

● **To the Parent**

Sunlight appears to be white but actually is a mixture of colours. If sunlight passes through a prism it separates into seven colours. The prism refracts, or bends, light at an angle that varies with each colour. Thus the red, refracted least, is at the top; and the violet, refracted most, is at the bottom. A rainbow appears when sunlight is refracted this way by millions of tiny drops of rain.

 Why Are There Different Seasons?

ANSWER Many countries don't get the same amount of heat all the time from the sun. In the summer season there is lots of heat, but there is much less heat in the winter season. Let's take a look at the northern countries' seasons.

■ Spring

In the spring there is more heat from the sun than there is in the winter, but it's not as hot as the summer. The weather is just pleasantly warm.

▼ The leaves of an elm tree appear in the spring and have a pale green colour.

■ Summer

In summer there is a lot of heat from the sun. It can be very hot.

▼ And the leaves of many trees have a lovely deep green colour.

■ Autumn

In the autumn there is less heat from the sun than in the summer but more than in the winter. So the weather is neither very hot nor very cold.

▼ In autumn most leaves turn red and yellow and fall to the ground.

Winter

There is only a little heat from the sun in the winter, so the weather is cold.

▼ The trees lose their leaves and sometimes are covered with ice.

● **To the Parent**

In the temperate zones there is a full range of four seasons. As the earth revolves round the sun, it rotates on an axis, which passes through the north and south poles. Because the axis is inclined at an angle of about 23.5 degrees, the amount of heat that is received in the temperate zones can vary greatly, from a lot of heat in the summer to only a little heat in the winter. Spring and autumn are mostly moderate.

Why Are Breezes Cool in Hot Weather?

ANSWER A person's body is quite warm. It's warm enough to heat the air around it so that the air also becomes warm. When a breeze blows, it pushes away the warm air, and cool air takes its place. That's one reason why a breeze feels cool when it blows on your skin.

Warm air

Breeze

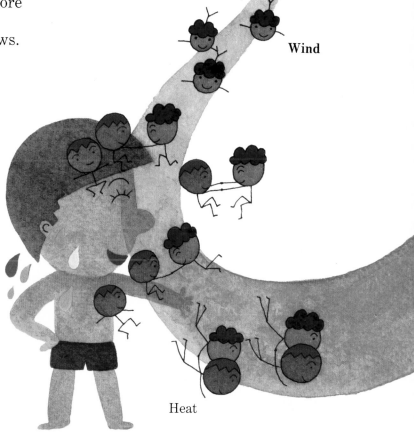

ANSWER When we're hot we sweat. Sweat carries heat from the body into the air. It does this as it evaporates, or turns into vapour. That makes us feel cool. When a breeze blows, sweat evaporates more quickly. So that's another reason why we feel cool when a breeze blows.

Wind

There's no breeze in the house and it's hot.

Heat

MINI-DATA

Washing dries faster when the wind is blowing

When the wind blows, the water in the clothes turns into water vapour quickly. That's why the washing dries faster on a windy day.

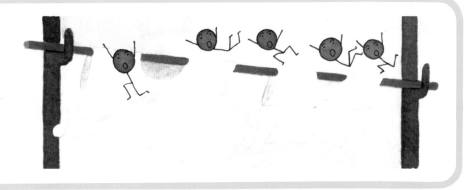

● **To the Parent**

The temperature of the body is almost always higher than the temperature of the air surrounding it. Perspiration cools the body by taking heat with it as it evaporates. This increases the moisture in the surrounding air, which reduces the rate of evaporation. But when the wind blows the humid air away perspiration begins evaporating more quickly again. For the same reason washing dries faster when it is hung in the wind.

Dec 2016 age9.

❓ How Does a Hose Help to Keep Us Cool?

ANSWER 1 If we sprinkle the ground with water, the heat from the ground warms the water. Because it's warm the water evaporates and rises. That makes the temperature of the ground and the air go down. And when the temperature is lowered, we naturally feel cooler.

The water that's sprinkled on the ground evaporates and takes heat with it as it turns into water vapour.

ANSWER 2 When water evaporates, it cools the air. The cooled air becomes heavy and moves around. The moving air causes little breezes, and those make us feel cooler.

● **To the Parent**

Our perception of heat and cold depends not only upon the temperature of the air but upon the wind and humidity as well. Even at an air temperature of 34° C., which is close to body temperature, we will not feel so hot if the humidity is low and perspiration can evaporate freely. The evaporation of water sprinkled on the ground sets up convection currents, and this motion of the air has a cooling effect on our bodies.

❓ Do You Know Why It Hails?

ANSWER High up in the sky it's very cold, even in hot weather. In the upper part of the clouds the water droplets freeze into tiny bits of ice. Those bits of ice become hailstones. Because hail falls very fast it doesn't have time to melt before it reaches the ground, even in hot weather.

Small particles of ice melt as they fall. By the time they hit the ground they are rain.

Ice particles

But How Do the Hailstones Grow to Such Large Sizes?

As ice particles get heavier, they fall. But inside some rain clouds there are very strong winds blowing upwards. The winds are strong enough to drive the ice particles back up higher. More water droplets freeze and stick to the ice pushed up by the winds. That forms larger particles of ice. When this happens again and again large hailstones form.

Droplets of water freeze onto the bits of ice.

They're driven up.

Strong upward winds

Large hailstones fall.

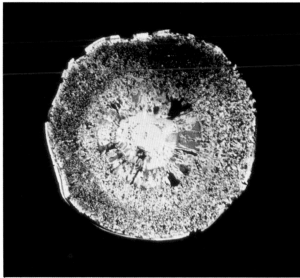

▲ If you cut a hailstone in half you see rings or layers, formed by water droplets that have frozen to it. We used a special microscope to see these colours.

▶ Some hailstones are so large they can break pine branches.

● **To the Parent**

Hail is ice pellets formed when strong updraughts in cumulo-nimbus keep the pellet suspended in the cloud as it accumulates more and more layers of ice until it is heavy enough to break away and fall to earth. Hailstones can cause much injury to livestock and damage to crops, homes and planes.

❓ Why Does Breath Turn White?

ANSWER The air we breathe out has a lot of water vapour in it. In cold places this hot, moist air cools in the cold air and turns into small water droplets. The droplets look white, something like mist.

Water droplets

Cold air

Water vapour

Places where your breath will turn white when you breathe out

In a warm room your breath wouldn't look white.

In the sunshine your breath would not be white unless it's very cold.

On cold mornings in the shade it would be easy to see your breath.

Why Does Steam from a Boiling Kettle Look White Even in Summer?

When water boils, droplets of water are turned into water vapour. This is called steam. Steam comes rushing out of the kettle, but the air can't hold all of that water vapour. Some of the vapour forms small water droplets, and those are what look white. They are hot, too!

● **To the Parent**

When the air can absorb no more moisture we say that it has reached the saturation point. The higher the temperature the more moisture the air can hold. But even on the hottest day, if too much water evaporates into the air it simply cannot be absorbed. When this happens the vapour that is not absorbed remains in the form of droplets, which appear as white mist.

What Makes a Shadow?

ANSWER When something gets in the way of a shining light, a shadow is formed.

If light comes from two places, two shadows will be formed.

I don't have a shadow!

If you run, your shadow runs too.

If you walk into a shadow, your shadow disappears.

Having Fun with Shadows

■ Don't step on my shadow

If someone steps on the shadow of your head, you lose.

Wait!

■ Shadow pictures

With a light in front of you, you can make shadow pictures. Make shapes with your hand, or by standing close to someone else.

Fox

Bird

Goat

Elephant

Dragonfly

● To the Parent

Light travels in a straight line. When it strikes an object it can not pass through, a shadow is produced. If the light source is weak, like sunlight on an overcast day, shadows are indistinct. In the shade there are no shadows. Shade is just the shadow of something already blocking out the light.

Why Do Shadows Get Longer or Shorter?

ANSWER As you move closer to the light, your shadow gets bigger. And as you move farther away from the light, your shadow gets smaller.

As you move away from the wall and closer to the light your shadow grows larger.

As you move closer to the wall and farther from the light, your shadow grows smaller.

If you're right under a light, your shadow will be small. As you move away from under the light, your shadow grows larger and longer.

If the light is just above you your shadow is small.

But see the shadow grow if you start to walk away.

Some shadows are coloured

If light shines on coloured jars or glass containers filled with coloured liquids, the shadows will be coloured too.

▲ The shadows of the caps are dark.

Why Is a Mountaintop Colder Even Though It's Closer to the Sun?

ANSWER The sun warms the surface of the earth first, then it warms the air near the surface. The warm air expands, or gets larger. When that happens, it rises high into the sky, where it cools. That's why the land lower down is warm but high up in the mountains it's cool or even cold.

Gosh, it's hot!

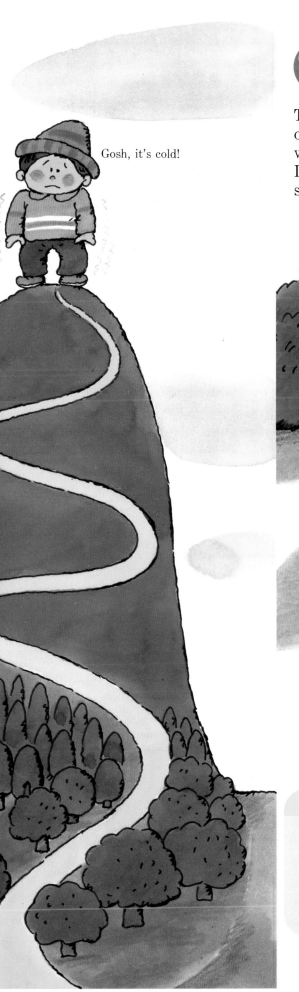

Gosh, it's cold!

Why Is It Cool In the Shade?

The sun's rays are what make it warm outside. When something gets in the way of the sun's rays, we have shade. It's cooler in the shade because the sun's rays aren't shining there.

A stone in a sunny place feels warm. But one that's been in the shade will feel cool.

● **To the Parent**

Objects or substances that absorb sunlight become warm. Sunlight does not have such a warming effect if it passes through something without being absorbed. Air is warmed only very slightly by the sun. When it is warmed, however, it rises, expands in the upper atmosphere and cools down again. As air descends, it is compressed and warmed. Up to 10 or 15 kilometres from the earth's surface the temperature of the air drops by about 0.6° C. for every 100 metres of increase in altitude. The low temperatures in mountains are due to combinations of these factors.

❓ What Are These?

■ Frost forming a column on a plant

In the winter, ice forms on a dry plant. It looks like a frost column, or frost pillar.

In autumn it blooms.

■ Ice on a tree

When it's cold in the winter, trees turn cold too. If the water vapour in the air touches a very cold tree it freezes and can look like this.

■ The aurora borealis

This is the aurora borealis near the North Pole. When electrified particles from the sun strike the air, colours are produced. There's an aurora near the South Pole called the aurora australis.

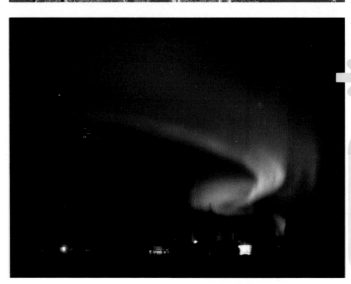

Growing-Up Album

Record of Reactions to Nature

Children experience surprise and wonder as they first encounter such natural phenomena as snow, rainbows or lightning. Record these moments here, along with your child's questions about nature.

● Rainbow

■Questions about Nature

Why is it cold on Mointon tops and warm on the ground?
Mountains

● Snow

● Thunder and Lightning

I like snow - unless it gets in my shoes!

● Ice

● Hurricane

Smudges' water ~~bou~~ in her
bowl Froze 1 cm thick.

■ Questions about Nature

Mount a photograph here

What Are These Signs?

Symbols such as these are used to show what the weather is like. Each symbol has a code mark under it. The picture with the same mark shows you what the symbol means.

♣ Thunderstorms

● Sunny

★ Sleet

♠ Fog

Weather charts — in newspapers, for example — have special signs that indicate different kinds of weather. Some are shown here. From the left, they are sunny, partly cloudy, rain, cloudy, thunderstorms, fog, sleet and snow.

▲ Snow

■ Partly cloudy

◆ Cloudy

♥ Rain

A Child's First Library of Learning

Weather

Original title: Nature

ISBN 0 7054 1031 5
TIME-LIFE is a trademark of
Time Incorporated U.S.A.

Editorial Supervision by:
International Editorial Services Inc.
Tokyo, Japan

Editor	C. E. Berry
Editorial Research:	Miki Ishii
Design:	Kim Bolitho
Writer:	Winston S. Priest
Educational Consultants:	Janette Bryden
	Laurie Hanawa
Translation:	Ronald K. Jones

EUROPEAN EDITION:
Gillian Moore, Ed Skyner, Ilse Gray, Eugenie Romer
Editorial Production:
Maureen Kelly, Samantha Hill,
Theresa John, Debra Lelliott

Photo, pages 48-49, courtesy of Japan Meteorological Agency

Typesetting by Compset Production Co. (H.K.) Ltd.
Printed by GEA, Milan and bound by GEP, Cremona, Italy

TIME LIFE CHILDREN'S LIBRARY